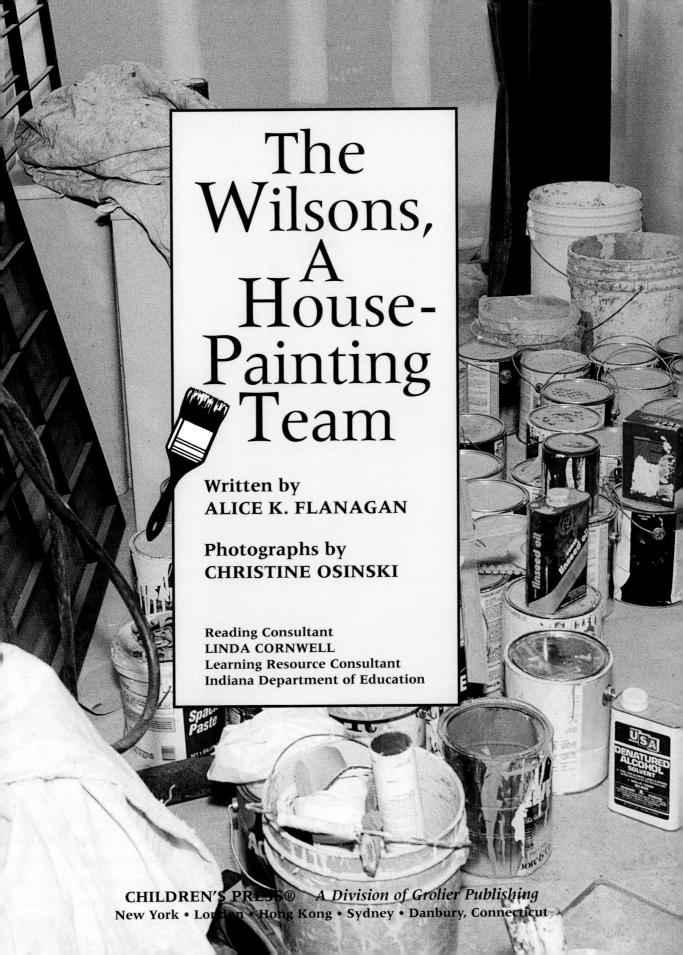

The Wilsons, A House-Painting Team

Written by
ALICE K. FLANAGAN

Photographs by
CHRISTINE OSINSKI

Reading Consultant
LINDA CORNWELL
Learning Resource Consultant
Indiana Department of Education

CHILDREN'S PRESS®   A Division of Grolier Publishing
New York • London • Hong Kong • Sydney • Danbury, Connecticut

Special thanks to the Wilsons for allowing us to tell their story.

Library of Congress Cataloging-in-Publication Data
Flanagan, Alice.
  The Wilsons, a house-painting team / by Alice K. Flanagan ; photographs by Christine Osinski ; reading consultant, Linda Cornwell.
      p.   cm. — (Our neighborhood)
  Summary: Describes the work of a husband and wife who own their own housepainting business.
      ISBN 0-516-20216-2 (lib. bdg.)—0-516-26063-4 (pbk.)
  1. House painting—Juvenile literature. [1. House painting. 2. Occupations.] I. Osinski, Christine, ill. II. Title. III. Series: Our neighborhood (New York, N.Y.)
  TT320.F53   1996
  698'.1—dc20

                                                        96-8603
                                                        CIP
                                                        AC

Photographs ©: Christine Osinski

Meet the Wilsons.
They paint and decorate houses.

They work as a team, using color and shapes to make homes look beautiful.

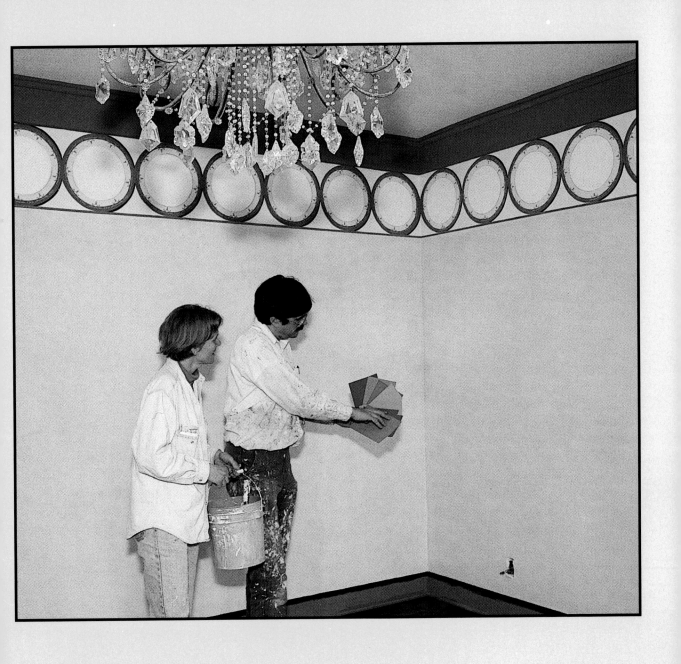

Before they paint a house, they plan
what colors all the rooms will be—

colors the owners might like
in different kinds of light,

colors that match things in the room
and are a pleasant sight.

After the colors are picked
and the paint is mixed,

the Wilsons bring brushes, rollers,
tape, paint, drop cloths, and
ladders, too.

They cover the floors and furniture.

11

They patch some holes
so all looks new

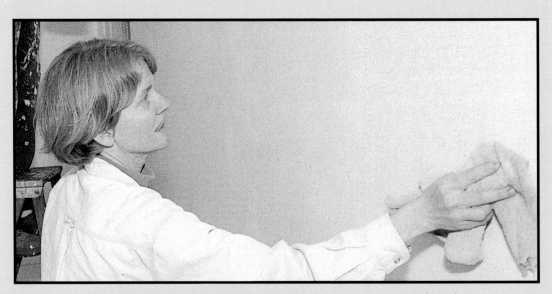

and wash off dirt and grease.

They scrape old paint
and sand the wood.

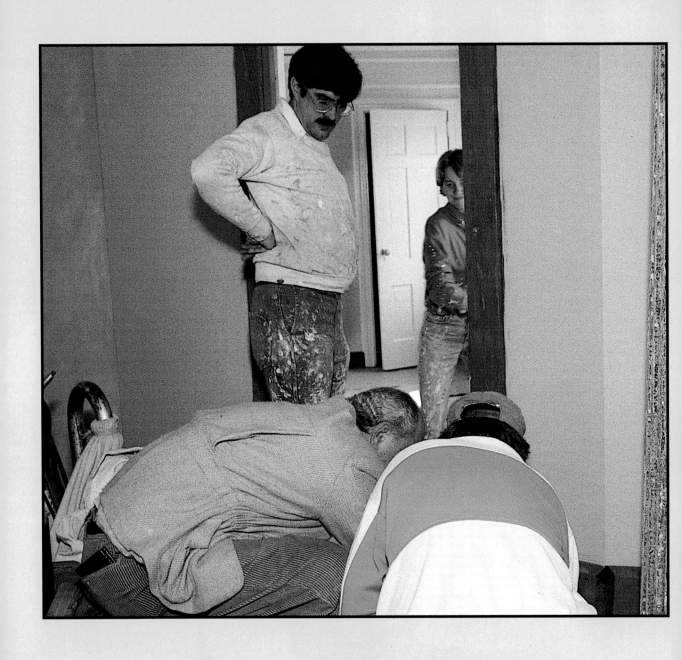

Sometimes they wait for work to be done by plumbers and electricians.

When all is ready, with steady
hands, they carefully start to paint.

First, Mr. Wilson paints the edge of the ceiling with his brush.

Then he spreads the paint with
sweeping strokes using a roller
on a pole.

He glides the roller
up and down the walls,

then finally paints the doors.

Mr. Wilson adds some details to make the rooms look bright.

He draws some designs
on a computer,

then traces them on the floor.

In another room, Mrs. Wilson works on the windows and the trim.

She also refinishes furniture.
It looks like new again.

For seventeen years, the Wilsons
have been painters.

They like working together and
doing the best that they can.

Running their own business
is hard work, but fun.

29

At the end of each day, they can look at what they've done and say, "We're helping the neighborhood."

"Our painting gives people a beautiful place to live."

Meet the Author
and the Photographer

Alice Flanagan and Christine Osinski are sisters. They grew up together telling stories and drawing pictures in a brown brick bungalow in a southwest-side neighborhood of Chicago, Illinois. Today they write stories and take photographs professionally.

Ms. Flanagan resides in Chicago with her husband and works as a freelance writer. Ms. Osinski is a photographer and teaches at The Cooper Union for the Advancement of Science and Art in New York City. She lives with her husband and two sons on Staten Island.